21st Century
Basic Skills
Library

WHAT DOES IT WEIGH?

by Cecilia Minden, PhD

Cherry Lake Publishing • Ann Arbor, Michigan

1

Published in the United States of America
by Cherry Lake Publishing
Ann Arbor, Michigan
www.cherrylakepublishing.com

Photo Credits: Cover and page 1, ©iStockphoto.com/hidesy; pages 3
and 4, ©broeb/Shutterstock, Inc.; page 4, ©Jim Hughes/Shutterstock,
Inc.; pages 4 and 6, ©iStockphoto.com/sjlocke; pages 8 and 12,
©Maxim_Kovalev/Shutterstock, Inc.; pages 8, 10 and 12, ©Finnbarr
Webster/Alamy; pages 10 and 12, ©Franck Chazot/Shutterstock, Inc.;
page 14, ©Hooyacrusty/Dreamstime.com; page 14, ©Digifoto Diamond/
Alamy; page 16, ©Elnur/Shutterstock, Inc.; page 16, ©Vera Volkova/
Shutterstock, Inc.; page 16, ©SRNR/Shutterstock, Inc.; page 18, ©Tyurina
Elena/Shutterstock, Inc.; page 18, ©swissmacky/Shutterstock, Inc.; page 18,
©dezign80/Shutterstock, Inc.; page 20, ©icyimage/Shutterstock, Inc.

Library of Congress Cataloging-in-Publication Data
Minden, Cecilia.
  What does it weigh?/by Cecilia Minden.
    p. cm.—(21st century basic skills library. Level 1)
  Includes bibliographical references and index.
  ISBN-13: 978-1-60279-849-6 (lib. bdg.)
  ISBN-10: 1-60279-849-4 (lib. bdg.)
 1. Weights and measures—Juvenile literature.
 2. Units of measurement—Juvenile literature. I. Title. II. Series.
  QC90.6.M56 2010
  530.8'13—dc22   2009048568

Cherry Lake Publishing would like to acknowledge
the work of The Partnership for 21st Century Skills.
Please visit www.21stcenturyskills.org for more information.

Printed in the United States of America
Corporate Graphics Inc.
July 2010
CLFA07

TABLE OF CONTENTS

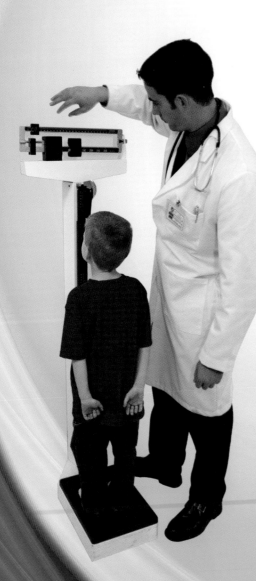

The Tools We Use

These tools help us **weigh**.

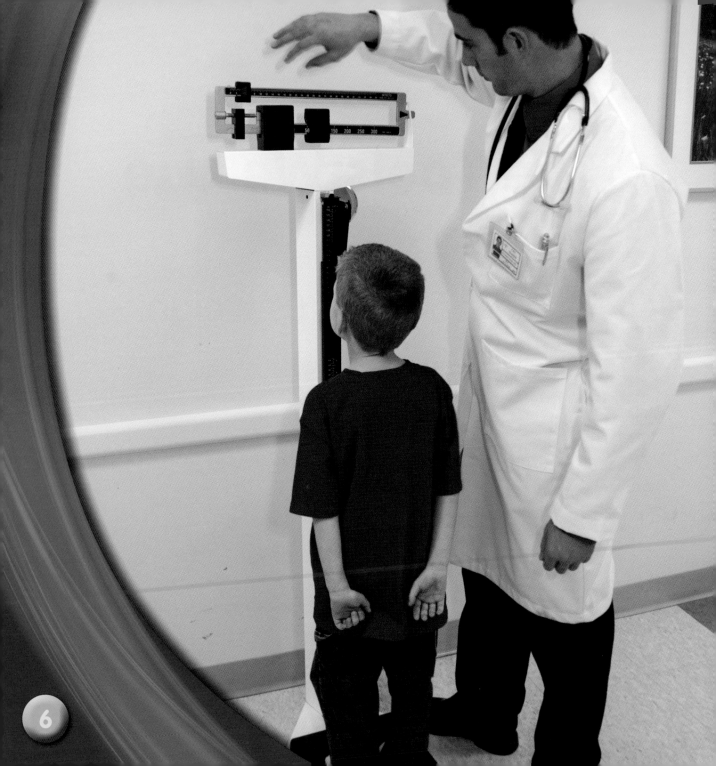

We use **scales** to find out how much we weigh.

We can use scales to weigh many things.

Ounces

The ball is small.

The ball weighs 4 **ounces**.

The frog is small.

The frog weighs 8 ounces.

Which one weighs more?

Yes! The frog weighs more.

16 ounces = 1 pound

Pounds

There are 16 ounces in 1 pound.

The butter weighs 1 pound.

The books weigh 20 pounds.

The apples weigh 3 pounds.

How much does the boy weigh?

How much does the girl weigh?

Step on a scale.

How much do you weigh?

Find Out More

BOOK

Aboff, Marcie and Francesca Carabelli (illustrator). *If You Were a Pound or a Kilogram*. Minneapolis: Picture Window Books, 2009.

WEB SITE

The World Almanac for Kids
www.worldalmanacforkids.com/WAKI-Home.aspx
Click on Weights and Measures to learn more about ounces and pounds.

Glossary

ounce (OUNSS) a small unit of measure

pound (POUND) a unit of measure; there are 16 ounces in 1 pound

scales (SKAYLZ) tools for weighing

weigh (WAY) to measure the weight of something

Home and School Connection

Use this list of words from the book to help your child become a better reader. Word games and writing activities can help beginning readers reinforce literacy skills.

a	frog	ounces	things
apples	girl	out	to
are	help	pound	tools
ball	how	pounds	us
books	in	scale	use
boy	is	scales	we
butter	many	small	weigh
can	more	step	weighs
do	much	the	which
does	on	there	yes
find	one	these	you

Index

About the Author

Cecilia Minden is the former Director of the Language and Literacy Program at the Harvard Graduate School of Education. She currently works as a literacy consultant for school and library publishers and is the author of more than 100 books for children.